Copyright 2010
Rights and Trademarks Reserved
THE MUSE
website: www.i-am-the-muse.com
email: muse@i-am-the-muse.com
No part of this publication shall be reproduced,
stored or transmitted in any manner except as permitted.
Sec: 107 or 108 of the 1976 United States Copyright Act.
Purchase control of these materials and works are under
the auspices of the publisher and the author.
Neither the publishing house nor the author shall be
liable for any personal or
commercial offense in regards that any reader may
experience through the reading
of the material including,
but not limited to special, incidental, consequential or other.
First Edition
ISBN-13: 978-1456390907
ISBN-10: 1456390902

Dedication:
To
Nanny Muse's
Heart-Keepers
(Who were all sprouts, once upon a time)

Welcome

to the Land of Enchantment,
deep in the southern wood.
Here, living is smooth and easy.
Words like "ought to" are spoken as "oughta" ~
and "want to" is voiced as "wanna."
Neighbors are your best friends ~
and there is always an adventure around the bend.
Miss Muse
is looking forward to visiting with you
at her little cottage by the "WATTA."

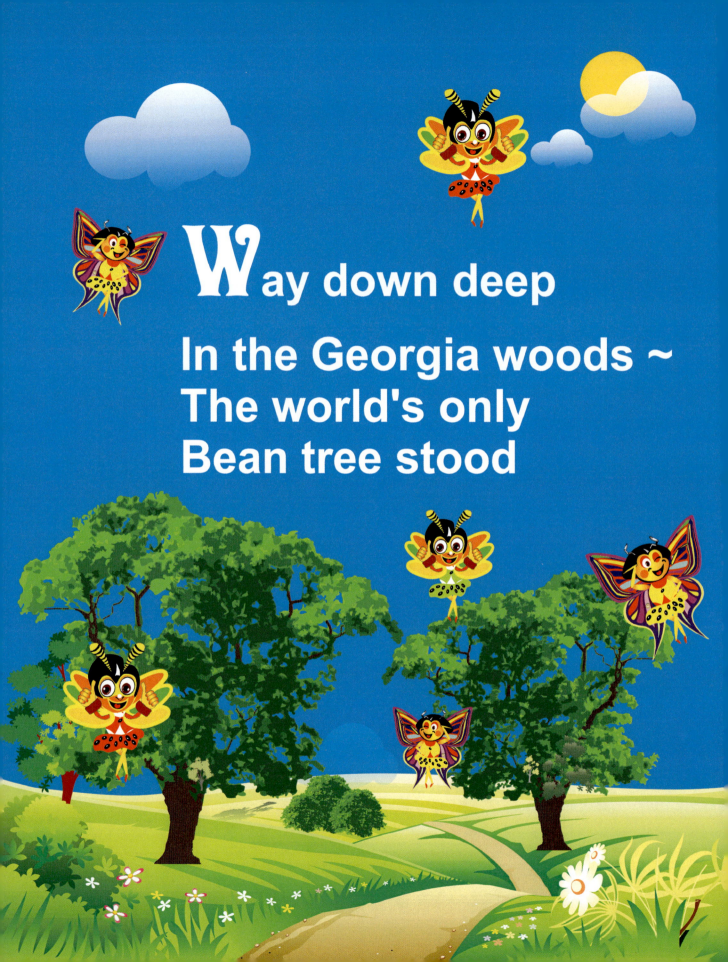

Her sweet kindness
Was akin to berries.
The woodland folk
Called the bean tree ~
Carrie.

One special day
She was given a gift.
A little seed so tiny
It needed a lift.

She gently raised
The seed with her limbs
Wanting to take
A good look at him

He yawned
And stretched ~
And opened his eyes ~
And his very first sight
Was the clear blue sky.

"Oh, I want to fly!"
He said with a grin.
"I want to soar and
Move with the wind!"

"Oh, no my love,"
Said Mother Carrie.
"You are a seed...
Not a dove!"

"Oh, I want to swim!"
He said with a grin.
"I want to feel wet...
I want to jump in!"

"Oh, tisk,"
Said Mother Carrie
"You are a seed...
Not a fish!"

Well, the little seed
Had quite enough ~
He turned around to be bold
He turned around to be tough ~

And then he saw her
For the very first time ~
His Mother the Bean Tree
With a tear in her eye.

And whippoorwills cried
A soft little sound ~
As she gently put him
On the ground.
And a Georgia breeze
Softly hummed a hymn ~
As he watched her supple
And mighty limbs.

You fly!" he sang,
As she moved to and fro.
"I wanna be like you ~
Mama, don't you know?"

And a Georgia rain
Pattered across the earth ~
And her roots drank it in
Giggling with mirth.

"Do you?" she asked him.
"Oh yes," he nodded.
"I'll do what you say ~
I'll do what I oughta."

"First", she said,
"You must sleep ~
And down the soil
Your roots they'll creep."

So, she made his bed
In the rich dark ground ~
And put him in softly ~
Cupping dirt gently round.

Mother Carrie,
The Bean Tree ~
Was the first to see
What had happened ~
To her little seed.

Made in the USA
Monee, IL
10 April 2021